BODY BY BISON
DIET AND RECIPE BOOK

Copyright © 2009 Tony Little

Book Creator: Jonathan Schwartz   Design & Editing: Daniel Koren   Art Direction: Tracy Ferguson   Photography: Chris Davis

Printed In The U.S.A.

Tony Little
The Story You Don't Know

For those of you who are not familiar with "America's Personal Trainer"™, Mr. Tony Little, you are about to discover the incredible power of change. For those of you that do know him, you know how truly POWERFUL his story is. Tony is the textbook definition of "Adversity to Victory". Tony has succeeded against all odds, with strong convictions and a deep caring for people. He has brought physical fitness into mainstream America that has enhanced the physical appearance, personal stamina and emotional outlook of his trainees.

In 1983 Tony was already an acclaimed Junior National Bodybuilding Champion, and ready for the big time. He was training for The Mr. America Bodybuilding Championship, the biggest competition of his life, which he was sure he would win. Then tragedy struck; a near-fatal car accident left him physically destroyed and emotionally crushed. Six months before the competition, Tony was blind-sided by a school bus. He had suffered numerous lacerations to his body and face. He also suffered two herniated discs, a cracked vertebra, a dislocated knee, not to mention the massive amount of soreness that he felt throughout his entire body from the devastating impact. Even though his body had been shattered, he still competed in the event and amazingly finished in fifth place. In the months following the accident, he slowly regressed into a depression which resulted in the slow death of the goals he had set earlier in life. Now, hooked on painkillers and a blurred image of his former self, nearly sixty pounds over-weight, Tony had hit rock bottom.

One morning in February 1985 Tony felt he had enough of the self-pity and downward spiraling. While he had felt "justified" in wasting his life, and blaming his circumstances on his current state, he knew in his heart that the only way to improve his situation was to take control of his life. That began with getting healthy, physically fit, and self-confident. Having spent many days watching various celebrities working out, promoting their gimmicks, diet fads and celebrity fitness videos, he was well versed on what America was being told about fitness, and he didn't like it. As a Certified Personal Trainer, Physical Fitness Specialist and former National Bodybuilding Champion, he knew there was much more to getting into shape than aerobic exercise. He also knew that physical strength and mental fortitude was the other half of the equation. So he developed a motivational non-impact resistance exercise technique that would reshape, redesign and re-strengthen the body with minimal joint stress. He knew all too well that poor physical shape is the first negative step toward emotional failures and he wanted to assure that his students were going to feel better and look better in a short period of time by exercising properly.

Tony believed in his idea and was determined to be successful. Armed with faith and confidence in his program, he drummed up his last spark of passion and drive. He went to find out what it would take to make an exercise television show where he could promote his one-on-one approach. A local cable company told him that it would take at least $15,000 to produce a limited local access program, so he started a company cleaning health clubs to raise the necessary capital. The show became an instant hit. Then, in 1987, Tony met the President and Founder of the Home Shopping Network. They struck a deal; if HSN™ could sell 400 of his videos in four airings, then they could work together on other projects. Tony sold all of his 400 videos in four minutes! His success was due to the fact that he was the first person to spend the majority of the time on his video discussing motivational exercise techniques along with muscle group information. Solid, sound advice became his trademark.

This opportunity catapulted his career to new heights. He had proven to himself that he had a personal training style that people were craving. Tony continued his quest to get America back in shape. In a very short time, he broke nearly every record at HSN™ for the personal training videos and equipment category. People were now starting to know who Tony Little was, his passion for personal training, and more importantly, his passion for people. While still working with HSN™, Tony decided to try and reach a larger audience by doing infomercials. In 1993, he had record-breaking infomercials in the United States and Europe. Tony then decided to team up with another major shopping network, QVC™, and like his time at HSN™, it didn't take long for him to start breaking records. Tony's life had become everything he had ever wanted professionally. He had numerous record-breaking sales for his videos and exercise equipment. He also had number one infomercials in several countries, won many awards, and of course, he was still doing what got him into all of this in the first place; helping people change their bodies and minds worldwide.

Life couldn't have been better for the blond haired, lean, mean, energized, personal training machine. However, in 1996, life threw Tony another curve. Yet again, he was involved in another life threatening car accident. His face was severely damaged, especially his left side. He had stitches down the left side of his nose, underneath his nose, down his lip, under his left eye, and several places on his cheek and jaw. He required more than 180 stitches and this accident took out two more lower back discs, now effecting 4 out of his 5 lower back supporting discs. Needless to say, Tony was worried about his well being and his career. Some people would have thrown in the towel after everything Tony had endured, but he just used this obstacle as another way to give himself the motivation to do what God had intended him to do: help people get in shape. In 1998, on New Year's Eve, Tony blasted through the record books. He sold over 200 tractor-trailer truckloads of his Gold Gazelle Glider™ on QVC™. That's amazing!

His devotion to help others, dynamic personality and energy level as well as his personal before-and-after story have made Tony a favorite among both the public and the media. He continues to capture the attention of audiences worldwide with his numerous appearances on popular TV shows including The Tonight Show with Jay Leno, Jimmy Kimmel, Ricki Lake as well as prominent news broadcasts on CNN and ABC World News Tonight. Tony has also been featured in such reputable print media as the Wall Street Journal, USA Today, The Los Angeles Times,

The New York Times as well as hundreds of health, fitness, general interest and celebrity publications.

Today, Tony is still breaking records as he continues to bring the fitness world new ways to get off the couch and get back in shape. His current accolades include 14 Platinum Video Awards, 9 Gold Video Awards and record-breaking infomercials throughout 81 countries. More than 40 million people worldwide have benefited from his exercise programs. In 2006, Tony was inducted into the National Fitness Hall of Fame. In 2008, Tony launched Body By Bison on HSN™. It became an instant hit and exceeded everyone's expectations. Without a doubt, Tony knows the formula to success. His life has been painful at times, but his attitude on overcoming obstacles is simple, "Conceive, Believe and Achieve™."

Tony, 26 years old, after his first accident

Tony today, 52 years old, after replacing his red meat with bison

You Can Do It !

America's Personal Trainer®

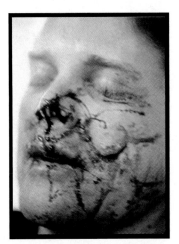

Tony, 39 years old, after his second accident

Table Of Contents

Introduction By Tony Little

Over the course of my career in fitness, a period spanning more than two decades, I have always tried my best to treat my body like a temple. Achieving this goal has taken countless hours in the gym, a positive, never-quit attitude and the willpower to maintain a proper diet. Regarding the diet, I have discovered one undeniable truth:

You are what you eat.

That's not my opinion, <u>it's a fact!</u>

This is why I'm a big believer in <u>bison</u>. And folks, I'm not just an endorser of it, I eat it every day. In fact, I've been eating bison for more than 25 years.

Now ask yourself this:

Would Tony Little, America's Personal Trainer, put something in his body he didn't believe in?

<u>No way!</u>

My quest as a champion bodybuilder in the early 1980s was to find a substitute for chicken and fish, which I was tired of eating all the time. That is what first led me to bison. I needed something that tasted great, had plenty of protein, was low in cholesterol and could keep me lean. That something was <u>bison</u>. After giving it a try, I was sold. Bison didn't just offer a better flavor than other meats, it was low in fat and helped give me the strength I needed to compete at a high level. Nutritionally, I was getting more protein and nutrients with fewer calories and less fat!

A car accident ended my bodybuilding career, but not long thereafter, I was pitching fitness products on TV. More than 20 years later, I'm still in great shape and bison is a big reason for that.

In this book, Dr. Kevin Weiland and I will show you how amazing bison really is. Dr. Weiland is a physician in South Dakota who has been a big advocate of bison for many years. He has helped countless patients lose weight by incorporating bison into their diets. His chapter on the benefits of bison will truly open your eyes and help you understand the importance of eating bison.

This book also includes simple exercises and tips to help you achieve your weight goal even faster.

Let's not forget the delicious recipes that will help you make bison part of your everyday life.

Speaking from experience, there's really nothing quite like bison. It is God's first real health food and now it's called a "Super Food". Let bison be your dietary salvation. I did!

America's Personal Trainer®

DR. KEVIN J. WEILAND
M.D., F.A.C.P.

THE BENEFITS
OF
BISON

Meet Dr. Weiland:

Kevin J. Weiland, M.D., F.A.C.P., is a practicing physician, board certified in the specialty of Internal Medicine. He is a graduate of the Sanford School of Medicine of the University of South Dakota and received his Internal Medicine training at the University of Wisconsin Hospital and Clinics in Madison, Wisconsin. He is an associate Professor with the Sanford School of Medicine and is actively involved in numerous non-profit organizations such as the American Cancer Society, American Heart Association, and the American Lung Association. Dr. Weiland is a fellow in the American College of Physicians and is identified as a leader in preventative medicine. He has been recognized with numerous awards for his community service as well as his ongoing work with school nutrition and childhood obesity. As a columnist, Dr. Weiland writes a monthly article on preventative medicine and has been published in the Annals of Pharmacology as well as the State Medical Journal. He is currently the "Supervising Physician" for the documentary movie Good Meat. Dr. Weiland lives in the Black Hills of South Dakota with his wife, Dr. Laurie Weisensee, and their children.

MY PATH TO BECOMING A PHYSICIAN

As an internal medicine physician, I specialize in the health care of adults. Like a pediatrician with children, I focus on adults. I have made a career of treating health problems that certainly include diabetes and heart disease. But I am lucky to be practicing medicine in this modern age when we can foresee, detect, and prevent disease before it overcomes the patient. Like many internists, preventive medicine is a major part of my practice. My journey to disease prevention actually began long before I started medical school. What I witnessed while growing up in a small town in South Dakota helped shape me into the physician I am today. My parents were hardworking owners and operators of a funeral home and ambulance service on the eastern side of the state. Back then, the local funeral homes typically provided the ambulance service since the hearse could easily transport the sick or injured to the hospital.

Not only did my father run the ambulance service, he was also one of the first emergency medical technicians (EMT) trained in the state. As an EMT, he had the necessary training in basic life support, but it was his experiences as a medic in World War II that gave him the confidence to care for the sick and injured. He was on call for our little community 24 hours a day, seven days a week, at a time when beepers and cell phones were pure science fiction. My mother served as his answering service and dispatcher. She alone had the responsibility of tracking down my father in the event someone needed his help. Needless to say, the Weiland Ambulance Service was an integral part of the community. Riding in the back of a hearse converted to an ambulance was quite an experience, especially for a 16-year-old boy. My job was to make the patient as comfortable as possible during the ride to the hospital. Just for the record, there is no comparing the smooth ride of a Cadillac hearse with today's ambulances built on the frames of one-ton trucks. To this day, I vividly remember helping my father transport one patient out of a muddy corn field. It was late in the harvest season, and the farmer had been working frantically to get the last of his crops out before the first snow.

When we arrived on the scene, he was sitting in an enclosed combine with his fist clenched tightly to his chest as he struggled to breathe. His skin was pale and his eyes had a blank stare of death. He was in his mid-fifties and extremely overweight, and it took several of us to get him on a stretcher and into the back of the ambulance. In the emergency room, the doctor began to perform a new procedure for the time, known as CPR (cardiopulmonary resuscitation). After several laborious hours, the doctor pronounced the farmer dead. The autopsy determined the cause of death was a heart attack (myocardial infarction) and found that several arteries were blocked in his heart. The report also noted that the gentleman had diabetes and high blood pressure.

All these years of assisting my father in transporting patients led me down the road of studying medicine, becoming a physician and helping people, just like my father did.

The world has changed since those days, especially in the field of medicine. We now have paramedics with special training in the pre-hospital care of the sick and ambulances are like rolling emergency rooms. Not only has technology improved the standard of care for the sick and injured before they get to the hospital, it has also saved countless lives as a result of advances in the care of an acute coronary syndrome such as a heart attack. Hospitals today are staffed with individuals trained to administer life-saving medications upon a patient's arrival.

The price tag for this type of care obviously has changed as well. While an ambulance trip in the 1970s cost $2, the same trip today could cost anywhere from $200 to $2,000. Emergency treatment for heart disease in the hospital can cost well over $20,000 for a single event—a tremendous expense for our society. What remains unchanged are the risk factors that lead to heart disease in the first place. Just like the overweight farmer I cared for long ago, obesity in combination with a sedentary lifestyle has resulted in as many as 50 million Americans at risk for premature heart disease and death.

I have dedicated my career to the prevention of disease and to educating my patients to practice a preventative approach, therefore saving them the expense and emotional toll of treating a disease. I have seen firsthand the diseases caused by our overindulgence in food as well as our sedentary culture. My hope is that in reading this book, you will gain a better understanding of why I am a big advocate of eating bison and how important it is to your health.

Our current state of unhealth is costing us, in dollars and in health:

- The number of workdays lost due to illnesses attributable to excessive weight amounts to 53.6 million days per year. Employers lose an additional $4 billion annually in lost productivity. (Shape Up America!, March1999)

- Over $100 billion is spent on medical expenses and loss of income due to weight conditions in the U.S. each year. This figure does not include the $47.6 billion spent per year to shed excess weight. (National Heart, Lung and Blood Institute, "Clinical Guidelines on Identification, Evaluation and Treatment of Overweight and Obesity in Adults," 1998)

- The health-care costs of treating seriously overweight adults in the U.S. in 1999 were estimated at $238 billion. (American Obesity Association, 1999)

- More than $51.6 billion is spent each year on health-care costs related to the cardiovascular complications of weight problems. (Shape Up America!, March 1999)

- Being overweight is associated with heart disease, cancer, high blood pressure, high cholesterol, and diabetes, which are conditions that lead to disability and death in the United States.
("Guidance for Treatment of Adult Obesity," Shape Up America!, American Obesity Association, 1999, pp. 16–23)

- One-third of all cases of high blood pressure are associated with weight problems, and seriously overweight individuals are 50% more likely to have elevated blood cholesterol levels.
(American Family Physician 1997; 55: 551–558)

- Gallstones occur three to six times more often in overweight people. Among women, 70% of gallstone cases are attributable to weight conditions.
(Shape Up America!, December 1995)

- Conditions related to being seriously overweight contribute to 300,000 deaths every year, and are second only to smoking as a cause of preventable death.
(Journal of the American Medical Association 1996; 276: 1907–1915)

- According to the American Diabetes Association, there are 16 million diabetics in the U.S. Of these, 15 million are type 2 diabetics, the form of diabetes that is closely associated with being overweight. ("Guidance for Treatment of Adult Obesity," Shape Up America!, American Obesity Association, 1999, p. 18)

- Overweight men are more likely to die of colorectal or prostate cancers than non-overweight men, and overweight women are at greater risk of dying of endometrial, gallbladder, cervical, ovarian, and breast cancers than women without weight problems.
(American Family Physician 1997; 55: 551–558)

Why Do Popular Diets Fail?

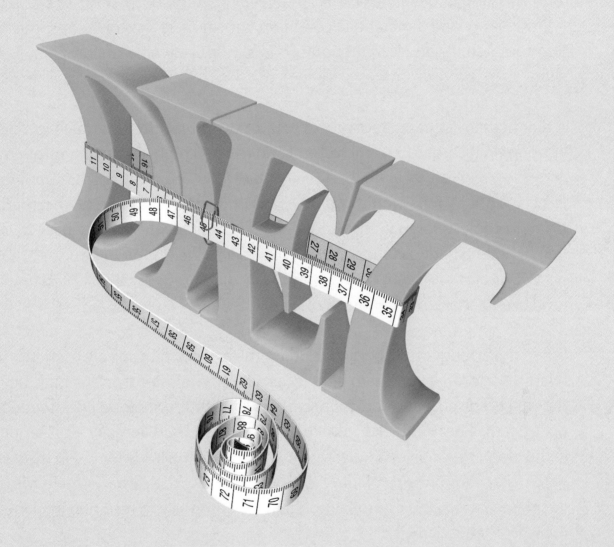

Over the past several decades, the general public has been exposed to numerous diets in its attempt to lose weight. Even though some people achieve their desired weight loss, many regain the weight after stopping the diet. The major problem I have with these popular diets is the fact that they are based on eating plans that are not nutritionally sound.

HIGH-PROTEIN, HIGH FAT DIET

One of the more popular diet trends has been the high-protein, high-fat diet. This kind of diet limits carbs so severely that the body starts to break down fat for energy and a metabolic condition known as ketosis develops. This diet is also too high in saturated fat and too low in fruits, whole grains, fiber, and calcium.

A diet high in saturated fats causes your body to produce too much low density lipoprotein (LDL or "bad") cholesterol and reduces high-density lipoprotein (HDL or "good") cholesterol in the body. Recently, I followed a patient's attempt to lower his weight by following this diet. As his physician, I was more concerned with his high cholesterol than his weight as he had a fairly lean body base given his height. Interestingly enough, he lost his desired weight of 10 pounds. However, his LDL cholesterol went from a marginally dangerous level of 123 to an unsafe level of 210 after several months of dieting.

When the arteries in the body (including the arteries that supply nutrients to the heart muscle) are exposed to high levels of LDL cholesterol after a high-fat meal, they are predisposed to constricting as well as clotting. If blood flow is reduced or obstructed, a heart attack or stroke often occurs. LDL is actually a carrier protein in the blood that delivers cholesterol to the cells in the body for use in the cell wall or to make hormones. If you have high levels of LDL, the carrier protein will dump its unused cargo (cholesterol) onto the walls of the artery, resulting in plaque formation (arteriosclerosis).

Another patient I recently cared for was told by his physician that he was "prediabetic" because of obesity. He was so upset by the news that he took it upon himself to lose weight. He followed the high-protein, high-fat diet and lost 10 pounds in the first month. I met him when he was admitted to the hospital and to my medical service with a condition known as acute pancreatitis. That morning, he had his usual large portion of bacon and eggs, but then developed abdominal pain. His pain was so severe that he had to be admitted to the hospital. His blood triglycerides (fats formed from the fats in food) were 10 times their normal level, causing his pancreas to react violently, becoming inflamed. The pancreas is the organ where insulin is produced. When inflamed (pancreatitis), pancreatic cells are destroyed and no longer able to produce insulin—as was the case in this unfortunate patient.

Another consequence of eating a high-protein, high-fat diet is that fiber is also severely restricted. Constipation can result if this very important food group is eliminated in the diet. Constipation can even flare up a diverticulum in the colon, causing a potential serious medical condition known as diverticulitis. Diverticuli are sacs or pouches within the colon that are formed when the walls of the large bowel are weakened.

HIGH-PROTEIN, LOW CARBOHYDRATE DIET

The high-protein, low-carbohydrate diet gained popularity in recent years. Again, the problem is in the amount of saturated fat consumed and that the diet is high in protein. Another patient of mine chose to eat a high-protein diet and, as a result, he developed acute gouty arthritis. Gout is an inflammatory condition of the joints in which a chemical called uric acid causes small crystals to form in the joint. These crystals are responsible for the inflammation and pain associated with acute gouty arthritis. The uric acid that accumulates in the blood and joints is a result of breaking down certain proteins consumed in the diet. The kidneys may also be affected, resulting in kidney stones made of uric acid. Most of the popular diets seem to focus on carbohydrates as solely responsible for weight gain and many of these diets feature high-fat foods. Granted, fat has been shown to give people feelings of fullness, resulting in less food consumed, but the health consequences from such a diet may be irreversible.

Low-Fat, High Carbohydrate Diet

Another very popular diet is the low-fat diet. This diet includes limited amounts of poultry, seafood, and meats, but generous servings of carbohydrates. Those who have tried it that I have spoken to found it very difficult to limit their fat intake. What many don't know is that not all fats are bad fats. Certain fats, such as omega-3 fatty acids (as those found in bison) can actually improve your cholesterol profile by raising the HDL and lowering LDL. Also, fat leaves the stomach very slowly, reducing food cravings. Thus, a certain amount of good fat may actually help you lose weight.

A SIMPLE SOLUTION

My wife (also a physician) introduced me to a healthy eating plan based on a nutritional program from the Island of Crete. It focuses on the health benefits of omega-3 fatty acids. After learning of this diet, the first thing that came to mind was bison. The meat of the buffalo (bison) that graze on the plains of the Dakotas has a lower amount of saturated fat and cholesterol and a higher level of omega-3 fats than their feedlot counterparts. I decided to develop a healthy eating plan for my own patients. My first test subject was none other than myself. By watching what I was eating and increasing my activity, I achieved the following:

> **I lost weight**
> **I lowered my total cholesterol by 25 points**
> **I lowered my bad cholesterol from 135 to 106**
> **I raised my good cholesterol from 45 to 61**

How did I do it?

I switched from eating beef high in saturated fat to leaner, grass-fed bison.

Fad dieting is just that—a fad that comes and goes as fast as your weight does. It seems all too often that society wants the "slim fast" program for weight loss. That's why the fad diet plans continue to be popular and these books continue to appear at the top of the best-seller lists.

My solution for weight loss is a simple one: **EAT BISON**

You will not only lose the necessary weight for ideal health, you will also improve your cardiovascular profile by lowering your cholesterol and blood pressure. I lost my weight the "slim slow" way by reducing my calories and increasing my activity. Eating bison was a big part of my success and by the time you finish reading this book, you will have an understanding of why bison truly is a "super food" and why I'm such a big believer in it.

BISON...THE SUPER FOOD

Imagine what Lewis and Clark witnessed as they trekked up the Missouri River and onto the open plains of the Dakotas during their famous cross-country expedition. It must have been an astonishing site for those early explorers, standing atop a hill and seeing tens of thousands of buffalo blanketing the landscape. At that time, the American bison (commonly known as the buffalo) numbered around 60 million and were free to roam most of the North American continent. The buffalo was the center of life and part of the spiritual culture of the Plains Indians.

This harmonious relationship between the Indian and the buffalo lasted for thousands of years. It took only a few decades of massive slaughter to leave the bison nearly extinct. The majority of the killings occurred between the 1830s and 1860s as wagon trains carted hides off to the east to be used in the production of clothing and belts. Hundreds of thousands of buffalo were arbitrarily slaughtered on a yearly basis, and by the end of the century, fewer than 1,000 remained.

In 1905, President Theodore Roosevelt convinced the U.S. Congress to establish a number of wildlife preserves for the buffalo. By 1929, almost 3,500 animals were counted. Today, the U.S. Department of Agriculture estimates that nearly 1 million bison exist throughout the United States and North America.

The bison, once a symbol of strength and unity for the Plains Indians, we now know to be a nutrient-dense food. The proportion of protein, fat, minerals, and essential fatty acids in bison is high in relation to its caloric value. When compared to other animals from a feedlot, the bison have a greater concentration of iron, omega-3s and other essential nutrients.

The meat from a grass-fed bison compared to a grain-fed animal has:

> **Less fat**
> **Fewer calories**
> **More omega-3 fatty acids**
> **More Vitamin E and other nutrients**

In fact, a 6-ounce steak from grass-fed bison can have up to 100 fewer calories than a 6-ounce steak from an animal whose diet was mostly grain. It is when live-stock are sent to the feedlot to be fed a grain-based diet that we see omega-3 fat and other nutrients drastically reduced in the cuts of meat.

Unfortunately, much of the meat produced in this country comes from the feed-lot. The food industry prefers this manner because it is relatively inexpensive to fatten the cattle with government-subsidized grain and they are able to produce massive amounts of the product year-round.

BENEFITS OF EATING BISON

The health benefits of eating bison cannot be understated. Here are a some important benefits which are the reasons <u>why I highly recommend eating bison</u>:

Great Source of Protein

Great Source of Iron

Great Source of Omega-3 fatty acids

Great Source of essential amino acids

Great Source of Vitamin B$_2$
(aids in wound healing, tissue repair and protects the eye lens from cataracts)

Great Source of Vitamin B$_6$
(protects against heart problems and promotes a healthy immune system)

Great Source of Vitamin B$_{12}$
(helps red blood cells work properly)

Improves learning

Aids in lowering cholesterol

Slows abnormal blood clotting in the body

Aids in having less discomfort during menstruation

Helps in preventing and/or controlling numerous diseases

HOW BISON CAN HELP PREVENT OR CONTROL DISEASES

Despite everything learned over the last several decades on obesity and disease, research into nutrition and health still lacks funding. Research efforts are focused on the treatment of diseases rather than prevention. At the same time, health-care costs in the United States are predicted to rise dramatically as the population ages. According to the U.S. government, one in every $5 will be spent on health care by 2015 and annual health-care spending will exceed $4 trillion. Common sense dictates that we implement a more preventive strategy, emphasizing healthier eating and exercise. What we now know is that eating foods such as bison can reduce your risk of developing a number of diseases:

HEART DISEASE

Labor Day in 1981 was the day my father passed away. He was only 55 years old, playing volleyball with his seven children while his only grandchild watched from the sideline. He fell to his knees, with a clenched fist to his chest, and passed away despite every effort to revive him. We could only assume that my father's sudden death was a result of a heart attack due to underlying heart disease. I was only 19 years old at the time, yet it was evident to me that my father had many of the risk factors for heart disease, such as smoking and a high-stress job. Little did I realize that his sedentary lifestyle and high-calorie diet would lead to central obesity, which alone is a major risk factor for diabetes and heart disease. It was decades of exposure to this type of lifestyle that led my father to his premature death.

In the years since then, we have gained a better understanding of the causes of strokes and heart attacks. As a result of expensive interventions such as heart catheterizations and bypass surgery, we have seen a decline in the death rate from heart disease. Yet, despite this wealth of knowledge, we still spend over $300 billion a year treating heart disease rather then preventing it from happening in the first place.

More than 600,000 deaths occur each year from heart disease; 1.5 million Americans will suffer a heart attack this year, and one-third of those people will not survive the event. The more risk factors you have, the greater the chances of suffering a heart attack, so take the necessary steps to reduce your risk of heart disease. You may prolong your life, but more importantly, improve your quality of life. Had my father changed some things in his life, he would be playing volleyball with his family today, and enjoying the quality of life many of his peers enjoy. Instead of one grandchild sitting on the sideline watching him play volleyball, there would be 17 grandchildren playing with him, admiring his youth and agility.

HEART DISEASE RISK FACTORS

Most physicians spend a great deal of time and effort educating patients on ways to modify those risk factors that lead to heart disease and strokes. Many patients take expensive medications in order to treat their high blood pressure or high cholesterol. The price of these drugs can be high, but so is their effectiveness. Newer and safer medications are constantly being developed. Taking these medications in order to lower blood pressure or blood cholesterol has been shown to reduce the risk of heart disease, strokes, and diabetes. The research into lifestyle changes is just as powerful. By exercising, eating the right amounts of fats, such as those fats found in bison, you may be able to significantly reduce the chance of developing heart disease.

There are unfortunately other risk factors for heart disease that cannot be changed but can be managed, such as the aging process and a family history of heart disease. The following is a list of risk factors and ways to slow down the disease process.

CHANGEABLE FACTORS

SMOKING

Smoking raises your heart rate and blood pressure, making more work for your heart. Plus, blood clots more easily and arteries constrict. Your heart muscle is more likely to have rhythm irregularities. There is evidence that nicotine (the chief addictive component of tobacco) directly affects the arteries by damaging the lining, accelerating arteriosclerosis. Quitting smoking will have an immediate benefit on your heart and lungs, not to mention your pocketbook.

HIGH BLOOD PRESSURE

You are at higher risk for heart disease if your blood pressure is greater than 135/90. Higher pressure means more work for your heart and damage to the lining of arteries, leading to a heart attack or stroke. If you are prescribed blood pressure medications, continue to take them, lose weight, reduce your salt and alcohol intake, and get regular exercise.

HIGH CHOLESTEROL

A total cholesterol greater than 200 and HDL (good) cholesterol of less than 45 places you at a higher risk for heart disease. Higher cholesterol in the blood causes a faster build-up of plaque in the arteries. Your target should be a total cholesterol of less than 200, triglycerides of less than 150, HDL (high-density lipoprotein) greater than 45, and an LDL (low-density lipoprotein or bad cholesterol) of less then 100. You can lower your total cholesterol by eating bison, as well as lower your LDL and raise your HDL.

EXCESS WEIGHT

More weight means more work for your heart and may lead to high blood pressure and diabetes. Reducing your total calorie intake by eating bison and increasing your daily activity level may help you avoid these problems.

STRESS

Negative thoughts and responses to stressful situations burden the heart with more work and make it susceptible to life-threatening rhythm irregularities.

LACK OF ACTIVITY

An inactive lifestyle at home or work increases your risk of heart disease. Begin and maintain a program of regular aerobic exercise. Walk more, use the stairs, and park your car in the farthest space in the lot and walk. You will be amazed at the health benefits of an active lifestyle and you may reduce your risk of a heart attack by as much as 50%.

UNCHANGEABLE FACTORS

AGE

Your risk for heart disease increases as you get older.

GENDER

Men are at greater risk for heart disease than women. This risk, however, is equal when women reach menopause.

DIABETES

Uncontrolled diabetes greatly increases heart disease risk. Weight loss and exercise can increase your body's ability to use insulin and glucose, causing some forms of adult-onset diabetes to disappear.

FAMILY HISTORY

If one of your first-degree relatives had their first heart attack before the age of 55, you are at increased risk for heart disease. It is imperative that you attempt to reduce the number of risk factors, such as quit smoking, lose weight, exercise, control your blood pressure, and control your blood sugars if you are a diabetic.

High Cholesterol

Did you know that the human body has over 60,000 miles of blood vessels? This network is like a river delivering nutrients and oxygen to our cells. When this blood vessel river flows freely, it efficiently transports its life-sustaining cargo, which helps keep our bodies healthy. If the river becomes blocked, illness and disease can occur because our cells do not receive an adequate supply of nutrients and oxygen. As we age, our blood vessels may become blocked. The blockage is often the result of hardening and narrowing of the arteries caused by plaques that build up in our arteries.

The main culprit causing this build-up of plaques is cholesterol. There are many factors that determine whether your blood-cholesterol level is high or low. Your genes might determine the amount of cholesterol your body makes, as high blood cholesterol can run in families. A diet high in saturated fats (found mostly in foods that come from animals) and trans-fatty acids (found in margarines and other processed foods) can raise your cholesterol level more than anything else. An important first step in lowering your cholesterol is to eat bison, which is low in these types of bad fats.

High Blood Pressure

An estimated 50 million American adults have high blood pressure and nearly a third of those don't know they have it. Some people may experience headaches or dizziness, but for most there are no symptoms at all. High blood pressure (hypertension) can go undetected for years, damaging your tissues and vital organs. If your blood pressure is not under control, your heart may enlarge and your arteries become stiff and less elastic. Eventually, you may not be able to pump blood properly, which can lead to congestive heart failure (backup of fluid into the lungs). Damage to your arteries can trigger a heart attack, stroke, kidney disease, vision loss, and shrinkage of the brain, resulting in memory loss and dementia.

When your health-care provider measures the pressure of blood in your arteries, he or she is listening for subtle sounds generated when your heart contracts to pump blood out (your systolic pressure or the top number). Between beats, your heart fills with blood again, generating the diastolic pressure (the bottom number). A normal blood pressure is usually less than 130 (systolic) and 85 (diastolic). New blood pressure guidelines suggest that people lower this even further to around 120/80.

Losing as little as 10 pounds can result in a significant drop in your blood pressure. Dropping weight is by far the most effective non-drug method of lowering your blood pressure. Eating bison can help you achieve the necessary weight loss. Bison is heart healthy because it is high in omega-3 fatty acids and monounsaturated fats (good fats) and contains little to none of the unhealthy fats seen in most processed foods. Several studies have shown that a diet rich in omega-3s can actually lower your blood pressure by 5 points.

ASTHMA

During an asthma attack, inflammatory substances known as leukotrienes are produced in the lungs. Physicians have an arsenal of medications that block the production of leukotrienes, which are eicosanoids from the omega-6 family. The omega-3 fatty acids have an opposing effect. Therefore, when eating bison (which is high in omega-3), an asthma patient will have less of the inflammatory eicosanoids that can make asthma worse and more anti-inflammatory eicosanoids. While medications are the mainstay of asthma therapy, eating bison will help you achieve better asthma control.

ALZHEIMER'S DISEASE

Autopsies have shown high levels of inflammatory substances known as inter-leukins in the brains of Alzheimer's disease sufferers. Interestingly, there are studies proving that patients with Alzheimer's disease have improved memory and mood when taking anti-inflammatory drugs. The goal in treating Alzheimer's is to reduce inflammation. This can be achieved with the right balance of omega-3 to omega-6 fatty acids. One study showed that those who ate a diet high in omega-3 (which is abundant in bison), had a decreased incidence of dementia.

CROHN'S DISEASE

Crohn's disease is an inflammatory condition affecting the entire gastrointestinal tract, from the mouth to the anus. The disease is manifested by abdominal pain, cramps, diarrhea, fever, and mouth ulcers, leading to weight loss and possibly even requiring surgery to remove part of the bowel that is inflamed. Crohn's disease is treated with medications that suppress the immune system, leading to a multitude of side effects. There are studies supporting a diet high in omega-3 fatty acids for keeping the disease in remission for a longer period of time.

ULCERATIVE COLITIS

Ulcerative colitis is another inflammatory bowel disease, which, unlike Crohn's disease, affects only the large intestine. Studies have shown that ulcerative colitis patients on medication need lower doses when they are on a diet high in omega-3 fatty acids. Eating bison is the perfect way to increase your omega-3 intake.

Systemic lupus erythematosus (SLE) is an autoimmune disease that affects every part of the body. This disease is made worse by the typical American diet high in refined foods and omega-6 fatty acids. Studies have shown that eating foods rich in omega-3 such as bison, helped those with SLE stay in remission for longer periods of time or use less of their medications in the treatment of the disease.

DYSMENORRHEA

Dysmenorrhea is painful menstrual cramps in women. During menstruation, the body sheds the endometrial build-up in the uterus, and inflammatory prostaglandins are produced. Women who suffer from menstrual cramps typically use drugs such as ibuprofen or aspirin to block the effects of the prostaglandins. Those eating bison (which is rich in omega-3 fatty acids) experienced less pain.

DIABETES

Despite the billions of dollars spent each year on weight loss and weight reduction products, obesity continues to be at epidemic proportions in the United States. As a result, we have over 33 million people with the type of diabetes seen in people who are overweight. Unfortunately, only about half of them know it. Type 2 diabetes is the most common form of the disease and it can develop over years, often without symptoms. It may reveal itself too late to prevent damage and many will learn they have the disease only when one of its most common complications develops -- heart disease, kidney disease, or vision problems.

Approximately 700,000 people are diagnosed with diabetes each year.

Diabetes can lead to a group of diseases with one thing in common—a problem with insulin. The problem could be either that the body doesn't make enough (or any) insulin or that it doesn't utilize insulin properly, thus preventing the right amount of blood glucose from entering the cells. The unused glucose will build up in the blood, causing a condition known as hyperglycemia. Almost all of the symptoms of diabetes result from persistent high blood sugars. Diseases associated with diabetes can affect almost every major part of the body. Diabetes can result in blindness, heart disease, strokes, kidney failure, amputations, nerve damage, and birth defects in babies born to women with diabetes.

If you have a family history of diabetes, your risk is increased. Unfortunately, being overweight at any age will put you at risk for developing diabetes.

Obesity is by far the greatest risk factor—80% to 90% of type 2 diabetics are overweight, which increases insulin resistance. Losing weight will allow you to achieve normal blood sugar levels without the use of expensive medications, which may have undesirable side effects. Achieving and maintaining a healthy weight is extremely beneficial and eating bison can assist in this goal. If you have diabetes, controlling your blood sugar is the single most important thing you can do to prevent disease.

Today, living with diabetes does not necessarily mean a drastic change in your lifestyle. By following a few healthy guidelines—eating bison, watching your weight, not smoking, and getting regular exercise—most diabetics can enjoy an active lifestyle and live a normal life span.

COLON CANCER

Colon cancer strikes nearly 135,000 Americans per year and is the nation's second-highest cause of cancer deaths, killing over 55,000 people a year. Tragically for many patients, a delay in diagnosis is the primary reason for the advanced stage of the disease at presentation and is associated with a poor outcome. You can lower your risk for developing colon cancer by eating plenty of bison and by limiting your intake of highly saturated fats.

MOOD DISORDERS

The brain is a fatty organ, with up to 60% of the mass of the brain composed of fat. Research is now showing a link between mood disorders, such as depression, bipolar disorder, dementia, and even schizophrenia, and a lack of omega-3 fatty acids.

Studies suggest that those who have a diet high in omega-3 fatty acids, which is abundant in bison, are less likely to experience feelings of depression or hostility. Researchers believe that those people who do not get enough omega-3 fatty acids are at risk for depression. Omega-3s are essential for maintaining mental health because they may help keep patterns of thought and mental reactions running smoothly and efficiently in the brain.

CONCLUSION

In America, the word diet or dieting can evoke a number of bad feelings. Many of us tried a diet, yet failed to lose the necessary weight or gained back what we lost and possibly more. Most of the popular diets are nearly impossible to follow, let alone maintain for any length of time. On the other hand, when we use the word diet in the phrase "healthy diet," we tend to believe that the foods involved are inaccessible or undesirable. Eating bison is not a diet, but rather a means to eating your way to a better life.

As you have read in the preceding pages, bison's health benefits are astonishing. This book was written to provide you with information on how nutrition can affect one's health and even prevent disease. The health implications of being obese are stark and clear. If you are overweight, you are at risk for just about every disease I describe in this book. Having an understanding of what can happen to the body as a result of these diseases will empower you to take action for your own health.

I want you to enjoy a happier and healthier lifestyle. My recommendation to you as a physician is to **start eating bison** for its tremendous health benefits as bison is the ticket to a healthier you.

DR. WEILAND'S SUGGESTIONS

Avoid processed foods and fast foods, as they are nutrient-poor and high in calories.

Eat protein with every meal. This will help you feel full and prevent you from having hunger pangs two to three hours after a meal.

Switch your regular consumption of fatty beef to leaner grass-fed bison. You could lose up to ten pounds the first year just by switching to bison.

Avoid all foods containing trans-fatty acids, as they will destroy your cholesterol profile.

Drink a minimum of 64 ounces of water daily. Drink one glass before every meal, as this will aid in weight loss by filling you up faster.

Eat often, at least five times a day, which will actually boost your metabolism and help you to burn more calories.

Don't skip meals. This will lead to overeating and extra calories between meals that will be stored in the body rather than used as fuel for the day.

Only eat sensible snacks such as bison jerky.

Avoid eating foods high in carbohydrates right before bed.

Exercise.

Get Fit In 10 Easy Steps

Exercise is so important to your body. This chapter contains 10 simple exercises to increase your muscle tone, improve your body's shape and speed up your metabolism for 24-hour calorie burning.

I have chosen these exercises as they can easily be performed in the comfort of your home. Before you can get started, you will need light dumbbells. Pairs of 3 pound and 5 pound dumbbells are great starting weights for women. I recommend 10 and 12 pound dumbbells for men.

Perform these exercises 3 times a week for maximum results. Don't forget to warm up before exercising by walking in place, marching around your living room or any other type of cardio exercise for 3 - 5 minutes.

Beginners should do 1 set of each exercise. Once you have advanced, you can increase it to 2 sets.

In addition, I recommend doing some low-impact cardio exercise. Pick your favorite form of cardio: power walking, cycling, using a Gazelle, Rock N' Roll Stepper or treadmill. Doing cardio 2 - 3 days a week will really get your body to burn fat. It is also great for your heart and lungs.

Also, don't forget to consult with your physician before starting any exercise program and follow your physician's recommendations.

What are you waiting for? **You can do it!**

01

full squat

TARGET:
Legs and Butt

1.
Use dumbbells for this exercise.

2.
Starting Position:
Stand with your feet shoulder width apart and knees slightly bent.

3.
Slowly lower yourself as if you were about to sit in a chair. At the same time, bring your arms out in front of you for balance. Go down as far as comfortable.

4.
Squeeze and push back up to the starting position.

SET ONE:
10 - 12 repetitions

SET TWO:
10 - 12 repetitions

A

B

TARGET:
Legs and Butt

1.
Use your bodyweight or dumbbells for this exercise.

2.
Starting Position:
Stand upright and take a large stride forward with your right leg.

3.
Bending your right knee, let your left knee trail as low as comfortable, but do not touch the floor. Keep your right knee over the ball of your foot.
(If it extends too far, your stride is too short. If it does not go over the ball of your foot, your stride is too long).

4.
Concentrate on the front leg pushing you back up. Stand back up to the starting position and squeeze. Finish all your reps for one leg before moving to the other leg to repeat this exercise.

SET ONE:
10 - 12 repetitions per leg

SET TWO:
10 - 12 repetitions per leg

stationary lunge

A

B

walking lunge

TARGET:
Legs and Butt

1.
Use your bodyweight or dumbbells for this exercise.

2.
Starting Position:
Stand up straight holding a dumbbell in each hand.

3.
Take a large stride forward with your right leg. Let your left knee trail as low as comfortable, but do not touch the floor.

4.
Bring your left leg forward until you stand upright again. Your position now should be a step forward from where you started.

5.
Take another stride forward, this time with your left leg (as if you are walking). Count each step forward as one rep and remember to squeeze up on each repetition.

SET ONE:
10 - 12 repetitions

SET TWO:
10 - 12 repetitions

A

B

TARGET:
Back and Shoulders

A

1.
Use a dumbbell and a sturdy, armless chair or bench for this exercise.

2.
Kneel on the chair as shown.

3.
Keep your chest almost parallel to the floor and your back straight.

4.
Keeping your upper body tense, squeeze the dumbbell up to the side of your chest, elbow slightly bent out.

5.
Slowly lower the weight down to the starting position.

B

SET ONE:
10 - 12 repetitions

SET TWO:
10 - 12 repetitions

back row with chair

chest crossover

TARGET:
Chest and Shoulders

1.
Use dumbbells for this exercise.

2.
Starting Position:
Hold a dumbbell in each hand and stretch your arms to your sides.

3.
Bring the dumbbells together in front of your chest with the right arm over the left arm and squeeze.

4.
Return to the starting position. Repeat with the left arm going over the right arm and alternate your arms for the remaining reps.

SET ONE:
10 - 12 repetitions

SET TWO:
10 - 12 repetitions

A

B

TARGET:
Shoulders and Arms

1.
Use dumbbells for this exercise.

2.
Starting Position:
Stand with your feet shoulder-width apart and your knees slightly bent. Hold a dumbbell in each hand and bring them up to shoulder height, palms facing away from your body.

3.
In a slight arc, lift the dumbbells simultaneously above your head.

4.
Slowly lower the dumbbells to the starting position.

A

B

SET ONE:
10 - 12 repetitions

SET TWO:
10 - 12 repetitions

shoulder press

07

tricep extension

TARGET:
Triceps

1.
Use one dumbbell for this exercise.

2.
Starting Position:
Position the dumbbell behind your head with your elbow facing outward. Use your free arm to keep the other arm stable.

3.
Slowly squeeze the dumbbells up above your head.

4.
Lower the dumbbell behind your head to the starting position.

5.
Finish all your reps for one arm before moving to the other arm to repeat this exercise.

SET ONE:
10 - 12 repetitions per arm

SET TWO:
10 - 12 repetitions per arm

A

B

48

TARGET:
Biceps

1.
Use dumbbells for this exercise.

2.
Starting Position:
Stand up straight. Hold a dumbbell in each hand with your palms facing forward.

3.
Squeeze your biceps and abs as you curl up the dumbbells.

4.
Lower weights slowly to your starting position.

A

B

bicep curl

SET ONE:
10 - 12 repetitions

SET TWO:
10 - 12 repetitions

ab crunch

A

1.
Starting Position:
Lie flat on your back with your knees bent and your feet flat. Rest your head on your fingers. Hold your elbows out to the sides and keep your chin pointing upward.

2.
Curl up and forward until your head and shoulders are off the ground. Make sure you are not pulling your head with your hands and that your chin is not touching your chest.

3.
Pause for a moment while squeezing your abdominal muscles. Make sure your back stays flat on the floor.

4.
Slowly lower your head back to the starting position.

TARGET:
Abdominals

SET ONE:
10 - 12 repetitions

SET TWO:
10 - 12 repetitions

B

reverse crunch

TARGET:
Abdominals

1.
Starting Position:
Lie flat on your back with your legs up in the air and your feet crossed at the ankles. Keep your hands under your lower back and look at the ceiling.

2.
Slowly lift your hips off the floor. Hold this position for a moment while squeezing your abdominal muscles.

3.
Slowly lower your hips back to the starting position.

A

B

SET ONE:
10 - 12 repetitions

SET TWO:
10 - 12 repetitions

TONY'S

TEN TIPS

As America's Personal Trainer and former body building champion, I have over 20 years of experience and knowledge when it comes to personal fitness. Over the years, I have developed 10 tips to help you achieve your goals even faster. These tips are simple, quick and easy-to-follow, yet very powerful. Make these tips part of your daily life. You will see and feel the impact in no time.

Tony Little

WATER
WATER
WATER

Water is the miracle of weight loss. I can't stress this enough. Drink it daily and drink it often. If you drink water before a meal, it will help you get full quicker. You can lose an extra 5 pounds per year by re-placing your sugary drinks with water. Water is a powerful way to cut weight so drink more of it.

TIP 1

TIP

SMALLER IS BETTER

Eat 4 to 6 small meals per day. This allows you to naturally raise your metabolism and makes you less likely to have snack cravings throughout the day. Try eating 1/2 of what you consider a good-size meal, and then eat the other 1/2 a few hours later. This will boost your metabolism, helping you burn more calories all day long.

TIP 2

TIP 2

EAT
LEAN PROTEIN
FOODS

Eat lean protein foods such as bison. It is the perfect food to lose weight. If you replace all your regular beef choices with bison, you can lose up to 10 pounds in a year. Other high protein foods include eggs, egg substitutes, turkey, chicken, fish and tofu for vegetarians. To maximize your weight loss, broil, bake, boil or poach your food and only use olive oil or non-stick cooking spray when cooking. If you are hungry in between meals, eat bison jerky. It is the perfect snack!

TIP 3

TIP 3

MINIMIZE HIGH GLYCEMIC CARBOHYDRATES

Minimize your consumption of high glycemic carbohydrates as they rapidly increase your blood sugar. These foods include white rice, sugar, pasta and potatoes. Eat low glycemic foods such as apples, grapefruit and multi-grain breads. Consuming less refined grains and eating more whole-grains improves insulin sensitivity, helps with weight loss, reduces body fat, lowers the risk for diabetes as well as cardiovascular disease.

TIP 4

TIP 4

57

EAT CARBS & PROTEIN TOGETHER

When consuming carbohydrates, pair them with protein and keep portion sizes small. Eating these foods together will keep you feeling energetic and satisfied until the next meal.

TIP 5

TIP 5

58

EAT HIGH-FIBER FOODS

Fiber is important to your diet. Foods containing dietary fiber include fruits, vegetables, nuts and grains. High-fiber foods make a meal feel larger and allow you to stay full for a longer period of time. Fiber also helps your digestive tract function properly and aids in reducing the risk of heart disease and diabetes.

TIP 6

TIP 6

BALANCE PROTEIN, CARBS AND FATS

When eating, the proper ratio of protein, carbs and fats will help you achieve lasting weight loss results. Try to keep your daily food intake at 40% protein (bison, chicken, fish), 40% carbohydrates (brown rice, yams) and 20% healthy fats (nuts, olive oil).

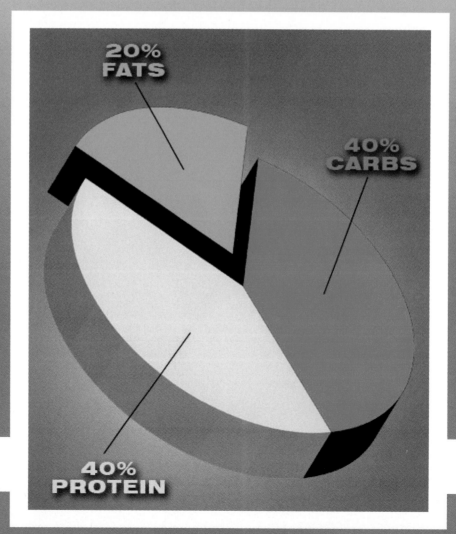

20% FATS

40% CARBS

40% PROTEIN

CONTROL PORTION SIZE

One of the key ways to lose weight and maintain a healthy weight is through portion control. The portion size of everything you eat should be the size of your fist. Protein can be more, but only if you're exercising. Americans often underestimate how many calories they are consuming each day by as much as 25%.

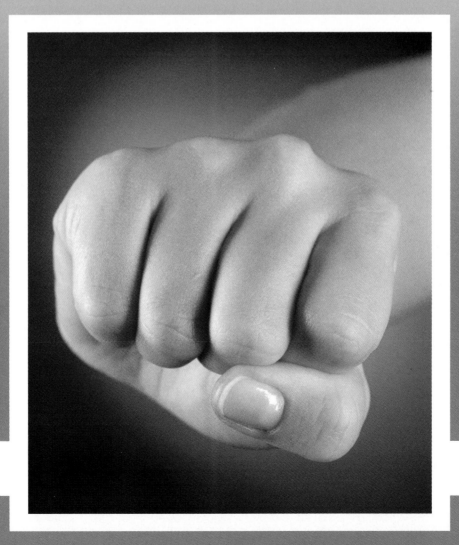

TIP 8

TIP 8

HAVE FOOD COOKED YOUR WAY

When eating out, remember to have your food cooked your way, which should be the right way. Remember, you're paying for the meal, so don't take "No" for an answer. Many restaurant foods can easily be adjusted to make them healthier. Have your food grilled, steamed or broiled instead of fried. Also, try to avoid condiments.

TIP 9

TIP 9

DON'T FORGET TO EXERCISE

Perform cardiovascular exercise 3 times a week for at least 20 - 30 minutes. Add resistance exercise from the previous chapter 2 - 3 times a week to increase your metabolism. This will put you on a fast track to your weight goal, so get off the couch and start moving!

TIP 10   TIP 10

Cooking With Bison
A Collection Of Recipes

When somebody thinks of bison, they typically think of a bison hamburger or steak. When I started Body By Bison, I was introduced to Jill Maguire. Jill has a long culinary career which began as a child on a South Dakota dairy farm and led to her ownership of 3 restaurants specializing in bison. Jill has spent countless hours in the Body By Bison test kitchen creating these amazing dishes.

The recipes are not only delicious, but also healthy for you. They were created under the supervision of a registered dietician. Each recipe states the approximate calorie and fat savings of preparing it using bison instead of beef. The differences will amaze you.

When preparing bison, remember that bison cooks faster than beef. Bison should not be overcooked or prepared to well-done temperature.

These recipes are easy to make and showcase how versatile bison really is. Breakfast, lunch or dinner, Jill created a recipe for it. Enjoy the great taste of bison and its health benefits every day with this collection of recipes.

All recipes were made with Body By Bison products available at hsn.com and bodybybison.com

BISON BREAKFAST SANDWICH

Makes 1 serving

1. Apply non-stick spray to a non-stick skillet.

2. Preheat skillet over medium heat.

3. Add egg, salt and pepper to skillet and cook for 2 minutes.

4. Using a spatula, flip egg over, top with cheese and add breakfast strips to the pan; cover and cook for an additional 2 minutes.

5. Place egg on half of the English muffin, top with breakfast strips and cover with the other half of the muffin.

6. Serve immediately.

Ingredients:
Non-stick cooking spray
1 egg white
1/4 teaspoon salt
1/4 teaspoon freshly ground pepper
1/2 slice low-fat American cheese
2 bison breakfast strips, cut in half
1 whole wheat English muffin, toasted

Save 110 calories and 23g fat

HEARTY BISON SCRAMBLE

Makes 1 serving

1. In a bowl, combine eggs, milk, salt and pepper; whisk well and set aside.

2. In a non-stick skillet, heat oil over medium heat.

3. Add peppers and onions to skillet; sauté for 3 minutes.

4. Add bison breakfast strips to skillet and sauté for 1 minute.

5. Lower temperature to medium-low and add egg mixture to skillet; cover and cook for 1 additional minute.

6. Remove cover and lightly scramble the egg mixture; cover and cook for 1 additional minute or until desired doneness.

7. Serve immediately.

Ingredients:

2 egg whites
1/4 cup fat-free milk
1/4 teaspoon salt
1/2 teaspoon freshly ground pepper
1 teaspoon olive oil
1/4 cup red bell peppers, diced
1/4 cup green onions, diced
2 bison breakfast strips, chopped

Save 110 calories and 23g fat

BISON & BULGUR WHEAT CAKES
WITH BLACK BEAN GRAVY

Makes 16 appetizer or 8 entree servings

1. In a bowl, combine bulgur wheat and water; cover and let rest for 1 hour.

2. Using a food processor, combine all gravy ingredients; mix well.

3. Transfer gravy to a saucepan on low heat; gravy will darken as it heats.

4. In a food processor, combine remaining ingredients except bison, oil, parsley and bulgur mixture; process well.

5. Add bison to food processor; while processing, add 2 tablespoons olive oil to the food processor.

6. Add bulgur and process; add parsley and pulse to incorporate.

7. Form mixture into 16 cakes.

8. In a sauté pan, heat 1/2 tablespoon oil over medium-high heat.

9. Place 8 cakes in the pan and cook for 2 minutes on each side.

10. Remove cakes and place on paper towels.

11. Add remaining oil to pan and repeat with remaining cakes.

12. Top cakes with black bean gravy and serve.

Ingredients:

1/2 cup bulgur wheat
1/2 cup warm water
1 small onion, chopped
1 teaspoon salt
2 teaspoons black pepper
1 teaspoon cumin

1 teaspoon allspice
1/2 teaspoon cinnamon
1 pound ground bison
3 tablespoons olive oil, divided
2 tablespoons fresh parsley, chopped

Black Bean Gravy:

1 can (15 ounces) black beans
1 can (5 ounces) crushed tomatill[e]
1 teaspoon salt
1 teaspoon black pepper
1 tablespoon lime juice

Save 115 calories and 22g fat

BISON WASABI LETTUCE WRAPS

Makes 5 appetizer servings

1. In a blender, combine peanut sauce ingredients except cilantro; puree.

2. Add cilantro to blender; pulse to incorporate.

3. Using a food processor, grind wasabi peas into a medium-fine flour.

4. Divide flour between two plates.

5. Season burger patty with soy sauce, salt and pepper; cut into 5 strips.

6. Press and roll strips in wasabi flour.

7. Preheat oil in a sauté pan over medium heat.

8. Add bison strips to the pan and cook for 4 minutes, turning often.

9. Remove strips from pan and place them on remaining wasabi flour; roll strips gently.

10. Add carrots and water to sauté pan; toss for 1 minute.

11. Arrange lettuce leaves, bison and carrots on a platter.

12. Serve with peanut sauce.

Ingredients:
1/2 cup wasabi peas
1 half pound bison burger
1 teaspoon soy sauce
Pinch of salt
1/4 teaspoon freshly ground pepper
1 tablespoon olive oil
1 cup carrots, shredded
2 tablespoons water
5 lettuce leaves, butter or romaine lettuce

Peanut Sauce:
1/2 tablespoon curry paste
1/2 tablespoon chili flakes
1/8 cup fat-free yogurt
1/8 cup peanut butter
1 tablespoon lime juice
1 tablespoon rice vinegar
1/2 teaspoon fish sauce
1 tablespoon water
1/8 cup fresh cilantro, chopped

Save 92 calories and 9g fat

4 BEAN BISON CHILI

Makes 10 servings

1. Preheat a heavy stockpot over medium-high heat; add oil.

2. Add bison meat to stockpot and crumble into small pieces using a wooden spoon; lightly brown for 4 minutes, stirring constantly.

3. Add onions, garlic and chili seasoning; cook for an additional 5 minutes, stirring constantly.

4. Add remaining ingredients, except vegetable juice; stir and bring to a full boil.

5. Reduce heat and simmer, uncovered, for 45 minutes or until desired thickness.

6. Add vegetable juice, stir until heated through and serve.

Ingredients:

2 tablespoons olive oil

2 pounds ground bison

1 large onion, chopped

2 tablespoons garlic, minced

1 envelope chili seasoning

1 can (28 ounces) diced tomatoes

1 can (29 ounces) tomato sauce

2 cups water

1 can (15 ounces) butter beans

1 can (15 ounces) black beans

1 can (15 ounces) kidney beans

1 can (15 ounces) pinto beans

3 tablespoons lemon juice

1 can (5.5 ounces) spicy vegetable juice

Save 184 calories and 18g fat

BISON GUMBO

Makes 12 servings

1. In a large stockpot, heat 2 tablespoons oil over medium heat.

2. Add stew meat, pepper, salt, garlic powder, onion powder, paprika, cayenne pepper, oregano and thyme to stockpot; cook for 5 minutes or until meat is lightly browned.

3. Remove meat from stockpot and set aside.

4. Add onions, peppers, celery and garlic to stockpot; sauté until tender.

5. Remove vegetables from stockpot and heat remaining 1/4 cup oil.

6. Add flour to stockpot; whisk for 20 minutes or until it is dark brown.

7. Add stew meat, vegetables and their juices back into the pan; stir.

8. Add chicken stock to stockpot; bring to a boil, cover, reduce heat to low and let simmer for 1 hour.

9. Remove from heat, let cool and refrigerate overnight.

10. Before reheating, remove oil that has formed on top of the gumbo.

11. Reheat gumbo over medium-high heat; stir, reduce temperature to low and let simmer for 1 hour.

12. Add shrimp and okra to gumbo, cook for 10 minutes and serve.

Ingredients:

2 tablespoons + 1/4 cup olive oil
2 pounds bison stew meat
1 tablespoon black pepper
1 tablespoon salt
1 tablespoon garlic powder
1 tablespoon onion powder

1 tablespoon paprika
1 teaspoon cayenne pepper
1 teaspoon oregano
1 teaspoon thyme
1 medium onion, diced
1 red bell pepper, diced

4 celery stalks, diced
1 garlic clove, chopped
½ cup flour
1 quart fat-free chicken stock
24 shrimp, peeled and deveined
3/4 pound frozen okra

Save 80 calories
and 9g fat

ITALIAN WEDDING SOUP

Makes 6 servings

1. In a bowl, combine all ingredients, except bison, stock, pasta and spinach; mix well.

2. Add ground bison to bowl; mix well.

3. Shape mixture into 40 small meatballs.

4. Place meatballs on a baking sheet.

5. Bake meatballs in the oven at 425 degrees for 8 minutes.

6. In a stockpot over medium-high heat, bring chicken stock to a boil.

7. Add pasta, meatballs and juices from the meatball pan to the stock; bring to a boil.

8. Reduce heat to low and cook for 8 minutes or until pasta is tender.

9. Add spinach to stockpot and cook for 2 additional minutes.

10. Ladle soup into bowls and serve.

Ingredients:

1 egg white, beaten
1/2 teaspoon fennel
1 teaspoon basil
1 teaspoon garlic, minced
1 teaspoon onion powder
1 teaspoon salt

1 teaspoon black pepper
1 tablespoon olive oil
1 pound ground bison
2 quarts fat-free chicken stock
1/2 cup orzo pasta
3 cups spinach, chopped and packed

Save 153 calories and 15g fat

GREEN CHILI STEW

Makes 10 servings

1. In a heavy stockpot, heat butter and oil over medium-high heat.

2. Add stew meat, chicken, onions, garlic, cumin, chili powder, coriander, cayenne pepper, salt and black pepper to stockpot; cook for 5 minutes or until meat is browned and onions are tender.

3. In a food processor, combine green chilis and red peppers; pulse and transfer to stockpot.

4. Add stock to stockpot and bring to a boil.

5. Reduce temperature to low, cover and simmer for 30 minutes.

6. Remove lid and simmer for an additional 30 minutes.

7. In a bowl, mix cornstarch and water together.

8. Raise stew temperature to medium-high and bring to a boil; slowly whisk in the cornstarch mixture.

9. Add remaining ingredients to the stew, stir well and serve.

Ingredients:

1 tablespoon unsalted butter

1 tablespoon olive oil

2 pounds bison stew meat

1 pound chicken breast, cut into cubes

1 medium onion, diced

2 tablespoons garlic, chopped

2 tablespoons cumin

2 tablespoons chili powder

2 tablespoons coriander

1 teaspoon cayenne pepper

2 teaspoons salt

1 tablespoon black pepper

3 pounds frozen green chilis, roasted and peeled

1 jar (15.5 ounces) roasted red peppers

1 quart fat-free chicken stock

1/4 cup cornstarch

1/2 cup water

2 cans (10 ounce each) diced tomatoes with lime juice & cilantro

1/3 cup cilantro, chopped

Save 96 calories and 10g fat

BISON MEATBALL SOUP

Makes 4 to 6 servings

1. In a bowl, combine all broth ingredients; stir well.

2. In a separate bowl, combine all meatball ingredients, except ground bison; mix well.

3. Add bison to bowl; mix well and form mixture into 24 meatballs.

4. In a large non-stick sauté pan, heat oil and water over medium heat.

5. Add meatballs to pan; cook for 5 minutes or until all sides are browned.

6. Add the bell peppers to the pan and cook for 3 minutes.

7. Add broth to pan; cover and cook for 5 minutes.

8. Remove the lid and add onions to pan; stir and cook for 1 minute.

9. Divide the rice noodles between 4 shallow bowls.

10. Add basil leaves to pan right before serving.

11. Divide meatballs and broth between bowls and serve.

Tony's Tip:
If you like it spicy, add a dash of cayenne pepper.

Ingredients:
1 tablespoon basil olive oil
1/4 cup water
1 yellow bell pepper, chopped
1 orange bell pepper, chopped
2 whole green onions, diced
2 cups rice noodles, cooked
1 cup fresh basil leaves, julienned

Meatballs:
2 teaspoons basil olive oil
1/2 teaspoon salt
1 teaspoon black pepper
1/2 teaspoon cayenne pepper
1 pound ground bison

Broth:
2 cups white wine
2 tablespoons red curry paste
2 tablespoons lemon juice
1 tablespoon brown sugar
1 1/2 cups water

Save 153 calories and 15g fat

BISON STEW

Makes 8 servings

1. In a large stockpot, heat oil over medium-high heat.

2. Add stew meat, salt, pepper, thyme and rosemary to stockpot; cook for 5 minutes or until meat is lightly browned.

3. Add sherry, 2 cups red wine and stock to stockpot; stir and bring to a boil.

4. Cover, reduce temperature to low and let simmer for 30 minutes.

5. Remove lid and raise temperature to medium-high.

6. Add onions, garlic, celery and carrots to stockpot; stir and heat through.

7. Let cook, uncovered, over medium-high heat for 45 minutes or until liquid is reduced by 1/3.

8. Add potatoes and mushrooms to stockpot; bring to a boil and cook for 10 minutes.

9. Combine cornstarch with remaining wine and whisk mixture into the stew; bring to a boil.

10. Reduce heat, add parsley and serve.

Ingredients:

2 tablespoons olive oil

2 pounds bison stew meat

2 teaspoons salt

2 tablespoons coarse black pepper

2 tablespoons thyme leaves

1 tablespoon rosemary

1 cup dry sherry

3 cups red wine, divided

1 quart fat-free vegetable stock

1 large onion, diced

2 tablespoons garlic, diced

2 celery stalks, sliced

4 carrots, peeled and diced

4 potatoes, unpeeled, parboiled and cubed

2 cups mushrooms, sliced

1/4 cup cornstarch

1/4 cup fresh parsley, chopped

Save 119 calories and 13g fat

TACO SALAD
WITH ZESTY SALSA VINAIGRETTE

Makes 6 servings

1. In a blender, combine all vinaigrette ingredients, except cilantro; puree.

2. Add cilantro leaves to blender and pulse until cilantro is lightly chopped; set aside.

3. In a sauté pan, heat oil over medium-high heat.

4. Add ground bison to pan, breaking the meat into small pieces using a wooden spoon.

5. Add onions, garlic, chili powder, cumin, coriander, salt and pepper to the pan; cook for 7 minutes or until browned, stirring while cooking.

6. Add salsa to the pan and stir to incorporate.

7. Divide the lettuce between 6 plates.

8. Arrange tomatoes around the lettuce, top with meat, olives and cheese.

9. Drizzle salsa vinaigrette over each salad and serve.

Tony's Tip:
To spice it up, add a pinch of cayenne pepper to the meat while browning.

Ingredients:

2 tablespoons olive oil

1 pound ground bison

1 small onion, diced

1 tablespoon garlic

2 teaspoons chili powder

1 teaspoon cumin

1 teaspoon coriander

1 teaspoon salt

2 teaspoons black pepper

1/2 cup salsa

1 head iceberg greens, torn

2 tomatoes, cut into wedges

1/2 cup olives, sliced

1/2 cup fat-free Cheddar cheese, shredded

Zesty Salsa Vinaigrette:

1/2 cup salsa

1/4 cup rice vinegar

1/4 cup olive oil

1 teaspoon black pepper

1/2 teaspoon salt

1/4 cup cilantro leaves

Save 153 calories
and 15g fat

MARINATED CHOPPED STEAK SALAD

Makes 4 servings

1. In a blender, combine all marinade ingredients; mix well.

2. Set aside 1/4 of the marinade for the vinaigrette.

3. In a large bowl, combine marinade and all salad ingredients, except salad greens and burgers; toss, cover and let marinate for 2 hours at room temperature.

4. Rub 2 tablespoons of the reserved marinade into the burgers patties; cover and let marinate in the refrigerator for 2 hours.

5. Using a grill on high heat, grill marinated salad ingredients until tender.

6. Grill burger patties for 4 minutes on each side for medium-rare or until desired doneness.

7. In a bowl, toss salad greens with reserved marinade and divide between 4 plates.

8. Arrange grilled vegetables around each plate.

9. Cut grilled burger patties into strips, divide between salads and serve.

Tony's Tip:
Serve with a slice of crusty whole wheat bread.

Salad Ingredients:
1 red bell pepper, cut into 8 pieces
1 yellow bell pepper, cut into 8 pieces
1 zucchini squash, cut into 8 ovals
1 red onion, cut into 5 thick circles
4 small portabella mushrooms
16 cherry tomatoes
8 cups fresh salad greens
2 half pound bison burgers

Marinade:
1/4 cup balsamic vinegar
1 tablespoon lemon juice
3 tablespoons sugar
1 tablespoon black pepper
1 teaspoon salt
1/2 cup olive oil

Save 230 calories

POTATO, APPLE & PEAR SALAD
WITH BISON STRIPS & WARM VINAIGRETTE

Makes 2 servings

1. In a sauté pan, heat oil over medium-high heat.

2. Add potatoes and onions to pan and cook for 2 minutes, turning once.

3. Add apples, pears and rosemary to pan; cook for 2 minutes.

4. Divide spinach leaves between two plates.

5. Transfer potatoes, apples and pears from the pan and arrange around the spinach.

6. Add bison strips to the pan and cook for 2 minutes.

7. Divide bison strips between the 2 plates and place them on top of the spinach.

8. Lower temperature to medium; add apple juice and mustard to the pan, whisk until incorporated.

9. Pour mixture over the spinach.

10. Top each salad with 1 poached egg and serve.

Ingredients:

1 teaspoon olive oil

1 red potato, boiled and quartered

2 red onion slices, halved

4 apple slices

4 pear slices

1 tablespoon rosemary, chopped

4 cups spinach leaves

4 bison breakfast strips, chopped

1/4 cup apple juice

1/2 teaspoon Dijon mustard

2 eggs, poached

Save 210 calories and 23g fat

FRUIT SPINACH SALAD
WITH BISON STRIPS & RASPBERRY VINAIGRETTE

Makes 1 serving

1. Using a blender, combine all vinaigrette ingredients, except oil.

2. While processing, slowly drizzle oil into the blender.

3. Place spinach into a bowl and drizzle 1 tablespoon vinaigrette over the spinach; toss until lightly coated.

4. Transfer the spinach to a plate and arrange the fruit around it.

5. Heat bison strips in the microwave for 1 minute, place them on top of the spinach and serve.

Tony's Tip:
You can substitute the fruit with your favorite kind of seasonally available fruit.

Ingredients:
2 cups fresh spinach greens
2 nectarine slices
2 peach slices
3 strawberries, halved
1/4 cup blueberries
3 bison breakfast strips

Raspberry Vinaigrette:
1/8 cup raspberry vinegar
1/8 cup raspberry jam
1/2 teaspoon black pepper
1/8 cup olive oil

Save 255 calories and 35g fat

BISON BLT SANDWICH

Makes 1 serving

1. Place breakfast strips between 2 paper towels and microwave for 1 1/2 minutes.

2. Season tomato slices with salt and pepper.

3. Spread mayonnaise on bread slices.

4. Top bread with lettuce, breakfast strips and tomatoes; cover with other bread slice and serve.

Tony's Tip:
Serve this sandwich with a
cup of tomato soup for dunking.

Ingredients:
4 bison breakfast strips, cut in half
4 tomato slices
Pinch of salt
1/4 teaspoon freshly ground pepper
2 teaspoons fat-free mayonnaise
2 whole grain bread slices, toasted
3 leaves iceberg lettuce

Save 420 calories
and 46g fat

PULLED BISON BBQ SANDWICHES

1. Gently pull roast apart and drain from juices.

2. In a pan over medium-high heat, combine pulled bison and BBQ sauce; toss and heat through.

3. Place bison on buns and serve.

Ingredients:

1 prepared bison chuck roast (2 lbs.), (see page 140), rinsed and patted dry

1 cup BBQ sauce

8 whole wheat buns

Save 147 calories and 18g fat

BISON HOT DOG KABOB
WITH CILANTRO YOGURT SAUCE

Makes 1 serving

1. In a blender, combine cilantro yogurt sauce ingredients (the recipe is on page 143); puree until smooth.

2. Assemble skewers by alternating hot dog pieces and vegetables.

3. Drizzle 2 tablespoons of yogurt sauce over the kabobs; let rest for 1 hour.

4. On a grill over medium-high heat, grill kabobs for 6 minutes or until desired doneness, rotating kabobs twice during grilling.

5. Top kabobs with additional sauce and serve.

Tony's Tip:
Serve kabobs over a bed of couscous.

Ingredients:

1 Jumbo Bison Hot Dog, cut diagonally into 6 pieces
1 small red bell peppers, cut into 1 1/2-inch squares
1 small orange bell peppers, cut into 1 1/2-inch squares
1 small zucchini, sliced 1/2-inch thick
1 small yellow squash, sliced 1/2-inch thick
4 baby portabella mushrooms

Save 118 calories and 12g fat

CLASSIC QUARTER POUND BURGER

Makes 1 serving

1. Rub oil on burger patty.

2. Season burger patty with salt and pepper.

3. Using a pan on medium-high heat, cook burger patty for 3 minutes on each side for medium-rare, turning while cooking (or cook until desired doneness).

4. Place burger patty on a bun; top with lettuce and tomato.

5. Serve with the condiments of your choice.

Ingredients:
1 teaspoon olive oil
1 quarter pound bison burger
Pinch of salt
1/4 teaspoon pepper
1 whole wheat bun
2 lettuce leaves
3 tomato slices

Save 230 calories and 22g fat

FORK & KNIFE PIZZA BURGER

Makes 2 servings

1. Brush olive oil on bread slices.

2. Lightly toast the bread slices.

3. Rub basil olive oil on burger patties.

4. Season burger patties with salt and pepper.

5. Using a grill on medium-high heat, grill patties for 2 minutes on each side or until desired doneness.

6. Place 2 tomato slices on each plate and top with olives.

7. Top tomato slices with cheese and microwave for 1 minute or until cheese is melted.

8. Pour warmed pizza sauce over toasted bread slices; top each slice with a burger patty and a prepared tomato slice.

9. Top with basil, drizzle with remaining olive oil and serve.

Ingredients:

1 teaspoon olive oil

2 whole wheat French bread slices

2 teaspoons basil olive oil

2 quarter pound bison burgers

1/2 teaspoon salt

1/2 teaspoon freshly ground pepper

4 tomato slices

1 tablespoon olives, sliced

2 low-fat Mozzarella slices

1/4 cup pizza sauce, warmed

2 tablespoons fresh basil, julienned

Save 230 calories and 22g fat

GYRO STYLE BISON BURGERS

Makes 2 servings

1. In a small bowl, combine relish ingredients; set aside.

2. Place 1/2 of the feta cheese on each burger and fold patty over, pinching edges together.

3. Rub olive oil on patties.

4. In a small bowl, combine remaining ingredients, except pita pockets.

5. Sprinkle mixture over both sides of the burger patties.

6. Using a grill over medium-high heat, grill patties for 4 minutes on each side, flipping twice during cooking (or until desired doneness).

7. Place burgers in pita, add relish and top with cilantro yogurt sauce (see recipe on page 143).

Ingredients:
1 ounce low-fat feta cheese, divided
2 quarter pound bison burgers
2 teaspoons olive oil
1/2 teaspoon black pepper
1/4 teaspoon oregano
1/4 teaspoon garlic powder
1/4 teaspoon ground coriander
1/2 teaspoon salt
1 whole wheat pita pocket per person, cut in half

Cucumber Relish:
1/4 cup cucumber, peeled seeded and diced
1/2 tomato, seeded and diced
1/4 medium red onion, diced
1/2 tablespoon lemon juice
1/2 tablespoon cider vinegar
Pinch of salt
1/2 teaspoon freshly ground pepper

Save 230 calories and 22g fat

CHOPPED BISON STEAK SCALOPPIN

Makes 2 servings

1. On a plate, combine flour, salt and pepper.

2. Place burger patties between 2 sheets of plastic wrap; press to half its thickness.

3. Remove patties from plastic wrap and place them into flour mixture to coat lightly.

4. Preheat oil in a sauté pan over medium-high heat.

5. Place patties in the pan and cook for 2 minutes on each side.

6. Remove patties from pan; cover with foil to keep warm.

7. Add butter to the sauté pan and let melt.

8. Add mushrooms to the pan and sauté for 4 minutes.

9. Whisk in wine and lemon juice; bring to a boil while whisking.

10. Place chopped bison steak over prepared pasta and cover with mushroom sauce.

11. Garnish with parsley and serve.

Ingredients:

1 tablespoon flour

1/2 teaspoon salt

1 teaspoon freshly ground pepper

2 quarter pound bison burgers

1 tablespoon olive oil

1/2 tablespoon butter

1/2 cup mushrooms, sliced

1/3 cup dry white wine

1 tablespoon lemon juice

1 cup whole wheat pasta, cooked

1 tablespoon fresh parsley

Save 230 calories and 22g fat

BISON MEATLOAF

Makes 8 servings

1. In a large sauté pan, heat oil over medium heat.

2. Add onions to pan and cook for 3 minutes.

3. Remove pan from heat, add garlic and stir to incorporate; set aside.

4. In a bowl, combine egg, Worcestershire sauce, 2 tablespoons ketchup, mustard, thyme, salt and pepper; mix well.

5. Add rolled oats and onion mixture to the bowl; mix well.

6. Add ground bison to the bowl; mix well and transfer bison mixture to an oiled loaf pan.

7. Bake in the oven at 375 degrees for 35 minutes.

8. Turn oven to broil, top meat loaf with remaining ketchup and broil for an additional 10 minutes.

9. Let meat loaf rest for 10 minutes before serving.

Tony's Tip:
Leftovers make a great cold sandwich.

Ingredients:

2 teaspoons olive oil

1 medium onion, diced

2 tablespoons garlic, chopped

1 egg

1 tablespoon Worcestershire sauce

4 tablespoons ketchup, divided

2 teaspoons mustard

2 teaspoons dried thyme

1 teaspoon salt

2 teaspoons black pepper

1/2 cup rolled oats, flash processed

2 pounds ground bison

Save 230 calories
and 22g fat

BISON STUFFED PEPPERS

Makes 6 servings

1. In a bowl, combine all spices; set aside.

2. Preheat a sauté pan over medium-high heat; add oil.

3. Add onions to pan; sauté for 2 minutes.

4. Add apples to pan; sauté for 1 minute.

5. Add bowl contents to pan; stir.

6. Add raisins and molasses to pan; stir well.

7. Remove pan from heat; let cool to room temperature.

8. In a bowl, crumble ground bison and add the onion mixture; mix well.

9. Divide bison mixture evenly between bell peppers.

10. Place stuffed peppers on a baking sheet.

11. Bake stuffed peppers in the oven at 375 degrees for 25 minutes.

12. Serve immediately.

Ingredients:

1 teaspoon cardamom

1 teaspoon cumin

1 teaspoon cinnamon

1/2 teaspoon cloves

1/2 teaspoon coriander

1 teaspoon black pepper

1 teaspoon cayenne pepper

1 tablespoon olive oil

1/2 sweet yellow onion, diced

1 large apple, peeled, cored and diced

1/3 cup raisins, soaked in the lemon juice

1 tablespoon molasses

2 tablespoons lemon juice

1 pound ground bison

6 bell peppers, tops removed and reserved, seeded

Save 153 calories
and 15g fat

CABBAGE ROLLS

Makes 8 servings

1. In a saucepan over medium heat, combine all sauce ingredients and let simmer for 10 minutes; set aside.

2. Remove core from cabbage center.

3. In a stockpot over medium-high heat, bring water to a boil.

4. Place cabbage into the pot and cover; reduce heat to low and let cabbage steam for 10 minutes.

5. Remove cabbage and peel leaves from head; set aside.

6. In a sauté pan, heat oil over medium-high heat.

7. Add ground bison to pan, breaking the meat into small pieces using a wooden spoon; cook for 5 minutes or until browned.

8. Add remaining ingredients to pan, except rice; heat through and remove from heat.

9. Add half of the tomato sauce and the rice to the pan; stir.

10. Place a spoonful of meat mixture in the center of each cabbage leaf and roll.

11. Place rolls in a 9x11-inch baking pan, cover with remaining tomato sauce and bake in the oven at 375 degrees for 30 minutes, covered.

Ingredients:

1 whole cabbage
4 quarts water
1 tablespoon olive oil
1 pound ground bison
1/2 cup green onions, chopped
1/2 cup Kalamata olives, chopped
1/2 cup pickled artichokes, chopped

1 tablespoon oregano
2 teaspoons salt
1 tablespoon black pepper
½ cup rice, cooked

Tomato Sauce:

2 cans (15 ounces each) crushed tomat
2 tablespoons brown sugar
1/4 cup lemon juice
2 teaspoons salt
1 tablespoon black pepper
1 tablespoon garlic, chopped

Save 115 calories and 11g fat

BISON & EGGPLANT CASSEROLE

Makes 8 servings

1. Arrange eggplant slices on a baking sheet and brush with 1 tablespoon of oil.

2. Broil eggplant in the oven for 4 minutes on each side or until lightly browned.

3. In a sauté pan, heat remaining oil over medium-high heat.

4. Add bison to the pan, breaking the meat into small pieces using a wooden spoon; cook meat for 5 minutes or until browned.

5. Add garlic, onions, salt, pepper and oregano to the pan; cook for 4 additional minutes.

6. Add tomatoes to the pan, mix well and let it reduce for 10 minutes.

7. Using a 9x13-inch pan, layer half of the eggplant on the bottom of the pan, top with sauce, mozzarella, basil and remaining eggplant.

8. Bake in the oven at 375 degrees for 30 minutes.

9. Top casserole with Parmesan cheese and bake for an additional 5 minutes or until cheese is melted.

10. Serve immediately.

Ingredients:

2 eggplants, sliced

2 tablespoons olive oil, divided

1 pound ground bison

3 tablespoons garlic, chopped

1 medium onion, chopped

2 teaspoons salt

1 tablespoon black pepper

1 tablespoon oregano

1 can (28 ounces) Italian style diced tomatoes

1 cup low-fat Mozzarella cheese, shredded

1 cup fresh basil, julienned

1/2 cup fat-free Parmesan cheese, shredded

Save 115 calories and 11g fat

BISON TACOS

Makes 6 servings

1. In sauté pan, heat oil over medium-high heat.

2. Add ground bison to pan and crumble into small pieces using a wooden spoon.

3. Add remaining ingredients, except salsa, lettuce, tomatoes, cheese and tortillas to pan; sauté for 7 minutes, stirring often.

4. Add salsa to pan and stir to incorporate.

5. Warm tortillas in the microwave for 30 seconds.

6. Fill tortillas with prepared bison, lettuce tomatoes and cheese.

7. Serve with salsa.

Ingredients:

2 tablespoons olive oil

1 pound ground bison

1 small onion, diced

1 tablespoon garlic

2 teaspoons chili powder

1 teaspoon cumin

1 teaspoon coriander

2 teaspoons black pepper

1 teaspoon salt

1/2 cup salsa

1/2 head iceberg lettuce, shredded

2 tomatoes, diced

4 ounces low-fat Cheddar cheese, shredded

12 whole wheat tortillas

Save 153 calories
and 15g fat

BISON ENCHILADAS

Makes 8 servings

1. Prepare bison roast according to directions on page 140 and gently pull meat apart.

2. In a food processor, combine cottage cheese and onions; puree and set aside.

3. In a small bowl, combine chili and tomatillo sauce; mix and set aside.

4. Apply olive oil cooking spray to a baking pan and pour half of the tomatillo mixture into the bottom of the pan.

5. To assemble enchiladas, divide cottage cheese mixture and bison meat between tortillas.

6. Roll tortillas and place them into the baking pan.

7. Top tortillas with remaining tomatillo mixture and cover pan with foil.

8. Bake tortillas in the oven at 350 degrees for 25 minutes.

9. After 25 minutes, remove foil, top tortillas with cheese and bake for an additional 5 minutes.

10. Serve immediately.

Ingredients:
1 bison chuck roast (2 lbs.), drained
2 cups low-fat cottage cheese
1/2 cup onions, finely diced
2 jars (16 ounces each) green chili sauce
2 cans (7 ounces each) tomatillo sauce
Olive oil cooking spray
16 corn tortillas, warmed
4 ounces low-fat Cheddar or Mozzarella cheese, grated

Save 147 calories
and 18g fat

ORANGE BROCCOLI BISON STIR-FRY

Makes 6 servings

1. In a large sauté pan, heat oil over medium heat.

2. Add ground bison to pan, breaking the meat into coarse pieces using a wooden spoon; stir gently.

3. Add jerk seasoning, chili flakes, salt and pepper to pan and cook meat for 5 minutes or until browned.

4. Add orange juice, onions, broccoli and snap peas to pan; cook for 2 minutes.

5. Cover and let simmer for 5 minutes.

6. Remove lid and add marmalade to pan; stir gently to incorporate and let heat through.

7. Garnish with cilantro and serve.

Tony's Tip:
Serve over a bed of brown rice.

Ingredients:

1 tablespoon olive oil

1 pound ground bison

1 tablespoon Jamaican jerk seasoning

2 teaspoons chili flakes

1/2 teaspoon salt

1 teaspoon freshly ground pepper

3/4 cup orange juice

1/2 cup red onions, chopped

2 cups broccoli flowerets

1 package (8 ounces) sugar snap peas

1/4 cup orange marmalade

1/4 cup cilantro, chopped

Save 153 calories and 15g fat

BISON FAJITAS

1. In a skillet, heat 2 tablespoons of oil over medium-high heat.

2. Add stew meat, salt and pepper to skillet; cook until browned.

3. Add tomatoes to the skillet and bring to a boil.

4. Reduce heat to medium-low, cover and simmer for 30 minutes.

5. In a separate sauté pan, heat remaining oil over medium-high heat.

6. Add onions and peppers to the pan; sauté for 4 minutes or until tender.

7. Transfer simmered stew meat and tomatoes to a platter.

8. Transfer onion and pepper mixture to the same platter.

9. Serve with warm tortillas and avocado slices.

Tony's Tip:
I love to top my fajitas with salsa.

Ingredients:

3 tablespoons olive oil, divided

2 pounds bison stew meat, rinsed, drained and patted dry

2 teaspoons salt

1 tablespoon black pepper

2 cans (10 ounces each) diced tomatoes with lime and chili

1 large sweet onion, cut into strips

1 green bell pepper, cut into strips

1 red bell pepper, cut into strips

16 corn tortillas

1 avocado, sliced

Save 119 calories and 13g fat

BISON BOURGUIGNON

Makes 8 servings

1. Preheat a heavy stockpot over medium-high heat; add oil.

2. Add stew meat to stockpot; brown for 3 minutes.

3. Add onions and garlic to stockpot; brown for 5 minutes.

4. Add brandy, salt, pepper, thyme, rosemary and basil to pan; stir well.

5. Add 2 cups red wine, stock, celery and mushrooms to stockpot; bring to a boil.

6. Cover and reduce heat to low; let simmer for 1 hour.

7. Remove celery, raise temperature to high and bring to a boil.

8. Add remaining red wine and cornstarch to stockpot, stirring constantly.

9. Garnish with parsley and serve.

Tony's Tip:
I love to serve this over whole wheat penne pasta.

Ingredients:

2 tablespoons olive oil
2 pounds bison stew meat, rinsed and patted dry
1 large onion, chopped
2 tablespoons garlic, chopped
1 ounce brandy
1 teaspoon salt
2 teaspoons freshly ground pepper
1 teaspoon thyme
1 teaspoon rosemary
1 teaspoon basil
3 cups red wine, divided
1 cup chicken or vegetable stock
1 celery stalk
2 cups mushrooms, sliced
1 tablespoon cornstarch
1/2 cup fresh parsley, chopped

Save 113 calories and 13g fat

ITALIAN BISON SPAGHETTI SAUCE

Makes 6 servings

1. In a heavy saucepan, heat oil over medium-high heat.

2. Add ground bison, onions, garlic, oregano, basil, Italian seasoning, fennel, salt and pepper to saucepan; cook until onions are golden and bison is browned.

3. Add remaining ingredients to saucepan, except spaghetti and basil; bring to a boil while stirring.

4. Reduce temperature to low and let simmer for 30 minutes or until desired thickness.

5. Serve over spaghetti and top with fresh basil.

Ingredients:

1 tablespoon olive oil

1 pound ground bison

1 medium onion, diced

3 tablespoons garlic, minced

2 tablespoons dried oregano

1 tablespoon dried basil

1 tablespoon Italian seasoning

1 tablespoon crushed fennel

1 teaspoon salt

2 teaspoons black pepper

1 can (28 ounces) crushed tomatoes

1 can (10.75 ounces) tomato puree

1 can (5.5 ounces) spicy vegetable juice

1 tablespoon balsamic vinegar

1 teaspoon lemon juice

1/4 cup red wine

4 cups spaghetti noodles, cooked al dente

Fresh basil

Save 153 calories and 15g fat

BISON & ARUGULA PENNE PASTA

Makes 4 servings

1. In a sauté pan over medium-high heat, bring water to a boil.

2. Add lemon juice, zest, salt and pepper to the pan.

3. Add pasta to the pan and stir well.

4. Cover pan and cook for 1 minute.

5. Add bison strips and oil to the pan; stir.

6. Cover pan and cook for an additional 1 minute.

7. Remove pan from heat.

8. Stir in basil and arugula; divide between 4 plates.

9. Top with freshly grated Parmesan cheese and serve.

Ingredients:

1/2 cup water

1 lemon, zest and juice

1 teaspoon salt

1 teaspoon black pepper

2 cups whole wheat penne pasta, cooked al dente

6 bison breakfast strips, julienned

1 tablespoon olive oil

1/4 cup basil leaves, julienned

1 cup arugula, julienned

1/4 cup fat-free Parmesan cheese, grated

Save 158 calories and 17g fat

SWISS STEAK WITH GREEN BEANS

Makes 6 to 8 servings

1. Cut roast crosswise into 3/4-inch steaks.

2. Rub 1 tablespoon oil into steaks; season with salt and pepper.

3. In an oven-safe skillet or heavy casserole, heat remaining oil over medium-high heat.

4. Add steaks to skillet and sear for 2 minutes on each side.

5. Repeat step 4 with remaining steaks.

6. Remove steaks from skillet, reduce heat to medium and add onions; sauté for 8 minutes or until lightly caramelized.

7. Place seared steaks on top of the onions in the skillet.

8. Add tomatoes, garlic, thyme, basil and oregano to skillet; heat through.

9. Cover skillet with an oven-safe lid.

10. Place skillet in the oven at 375 degrees for 45 minutes.

11. Add green beans to the skillet and cook for an additional 15 minutes.

12. Serve immediately.

Ingredients:

1 bison chuck roast (2 lbs.)

2 tablespoons olive oil, divided

2 teaspoons salt

1 tablespoon freshly ground pepper

2 medium onions, halved and sliced thick

2 cans (14.5 ounces each) diced tomatoes

2 tablespoons garlic, chopped

2 teaspoons thyme

2 teaspoons basil

2 teaspoons oregano

1 pound fresh green beans, washed and clipped

Save 147 calories
and 18g fat

MARINATED BISON STEAKS
WITH WHISKEY PLUM SAUCE

Makes 4 servings

1. Combine all marinade ingredients in a quart-size zipper bag.

2. Add steaks to the zipper bag; seal and massage marinade into the steaks.

3. Let marinate in the refrigerator for 4 hours.

4. Rest steaks at room temperature for 2 hours before cooking.

5. Remove steaks from marinade and pat dry.

6. Rub oil, salt and pepper into the steaks.

7. Using a grill on high heat, grill steaks for 2 minutes on each side for medium-rare or until desired doneness.

8. Top steaks with whiskey plum sauce (the recipe is on page 143).

9. Serve immediately.

Ingredients:
4 bison steaks (4 ounces each)
1 teaspoon olive oil
1/2 teaspoon salt
1 teaspoon freshly ground pepper

Marinade:
1 teaspoon black pepper
1/2 teaspoon salt
1 teaspoon fresh ginger, chopped
1/4 cup rice vinegar
2 tablespoons honey
1/2 teaspoon lemon juice

Save 133 calories and 15g fat

BISON STEAKS
WITH CHIMICHURRI SAUCE

Makes 4 servings

1. Using a blender, combine all sauce ingredients; puree.

2. Pour half the sauce into a bowl and add the steaks.

3. Cover bowl and let steaks marinate in the refrigerator for 4 hours.

4. Rest steaks at room temperature for 2 hours before cooking.

5. Remove steaks from chimichurri sauce and pat dry.

6. Rub oil, salt and pepper into the steaks.

7. Using a grill on high heat, grill steaks for 2 minutes on each side for medium-rare or until desired doneness.

8. Serve with remaining chimichurri sauce.

Ingredients:
4 bison steaks (4 ounces each)
1 teaspoon olive oil
1/2 teaspoon salt
1 teaspoon freshly ground pepper

Chimichurri Sauce:
1 cup fresh parsley, coarsely chopped
1/2 tablespoon oregano
1/2 tablespoon black pepper
1/2 tablespoon chili flakes
1/2 teaspoon salt
2 tablespoons garlic
1 teaspoon lemon juice
1/3 cup white wine vinegar
1/3 cup olive oil

Save 133 calories and 15g fat

GRILLED CHUCK STEAKS
WITH CABERNET SAUVIGNON SAGE SAUCE

Makes 7 servings

1. In a bowl, combine all marinade ingredients; whisk well.

2. Cut roast crosswise into seven 1/2-inch thick steaks, removing any large amounts of fat.

3. Place steaks in a gallon-size zipper bag and pour marinade into the bag; let marinate in the refrigerator overnight.

4. Before cooking, let steaks rest at room temperature for 2 hours.

5. Remove steaks from marinade and pat them dry.

6. Rub oil, salt and pepper into steaks.

7. Using a grill on high heat, grill steaks for 5 minutes on each side for medium rare (or until desired doneness).

8. Serve with cabernet sauvignon sage sauce (see recipe on page 142).

Ingredients:
1 bison chuck roast (2 lbs.), rinsed and patted dry
2 tablespoons olive oil
1 teaspoon salt
2 teaspoons freshly ground pepper

Marinade:
1/4 cup olive oil
1 bottle (12 ounces) beer
1/4 cup lemon juice
1 tablespoon onion powder
1 tablespoon garlic powder
1 tablespoon black pepper
1 teaspoon salt

Save 168 calories and 20g fat

Makes 6 to 8 servings

1. In a bowl, combine oil, salt, pepper, garlic powder, onion powder, thyme and rosemary; mix well.

2. Rub oil mixture into the chuck roast and place roast on roasting rack.

3. Pour wine and stock into a roasting pan and fit pan with the rack.

4. Cook roast at 375 degrees in the convection oven for 40 minutes for medium-rare or until desired doneness. For the best results, use a meat thermometer and cook until desired doneness.

5. Remove roast from oven and let rest for 10 minutes.

6. Remove twine from roast.

7. Thinly slice the roast and serve.

Tony's Tip:
Serve roast with horseradish cream sauce, the recipe is on page 142.

Ingredients:

2 tablespoons olive oil

1 tablespoon salt

2 teaspoons freshly ground pepper

1 teaspoon garlic powder

1 teaspoon onion powder

1 teaspoon thyme

1 teaspoon rosemary

1 bison chuck roast (2 lbs.), twine-tied, rinsed and patted dry

1/2 cup red cooking wine

1/2 cup vegetable stock

Save 147 calories and 18g fat

APPLE CIDER CHUCK ROAST

Makes 6 to 8 servings

1. In a small bowl, combine 1 tablespoon oil, salt and pepper; rub into roast.

2. In a heavy stockpot over medium-high heat, add remaining oil and sear roast for 2 minutes on each side, keeping one edge of the roast on the side of the pan.

3. Add apple cider to the stockpot; bring to a boil.

4. Cover stockpot and reduce heat to low.

5. Let roast braise for 2 hours, turning twice during braising.

6. Braising is complete when roast is tender (if roast is not tender, add 30 minutes to braising time).

7. Remove roast from heat and let rest, covered, at room temperature for 30 minutes.

8. Serve with juices from the stockpot.

Ingredients:

2 tablespoons olive oil, divided

1 teaspoon salt

2 teaspoons freshly ground pepper

1 bison chuck roast (2 lbs.), rinsed and patted dry

2/3 cup organic apple cider, warmed

Save 147 calories
and 18g fat

CABERNET SAUVIGNON SAGE SAUCE

Ingredients:

1 tablespoon butter

1/2 small onion, chopped

1/2 cup mushrooms, sliced

1 celery stalk, diced

1 tomato, chopped

1 teaspoon salt

2 teaspoons freshly ground pepper

1 tablespoon sage

1 tablespoon thyme

2 cups cabernet wine

1 1/2 cups fat-free beef stock

2 tablespoons water

1 teaspoon cornstarch

1. In a saucepan over medium-high heat, melt butter.
2. Add onions, mushrooms, celery, tomato, salt, pepper, sage and thyme; sauté for 5 minutes.
3. Add cabernet and stock to saucepan; bring to a boil.
4. Reduce heat to low and let simmer until reduced to half.
5. Strain sauce using a strainer; discard vegetables.
6. In a small bowl, combine water and cornstarch.
7. Return sauce to stove top over medium-high heat and whisk in the cornstarch mixture.
8. Serve over steaks, roasts or meatloaf.

HORSERADISH CREAM SAUCE

Ingredients:

1/4 cup fat-free sour cream

1/8 cup prepared horseradish

1/2 tablespoon Worcestershire sauce

Pinch of salt

1/2 teaspoon black pepper

1. In a bowl, combine all ingredients; mix well.

WHISKEY PLUM SAUCE

Ingredients:

1 tablespoon salted butter

1/4 cup green onions, finely chopped

1/2 teaspoon salt

1 teaspoon black pepper

1/4 cup plum jam

1/4 cup whiskey

1. In a saucepan over medium heat, melt butter.
2. Add green onions to saucepan; cook for 3 minutes.
3. Add salt, pepper and plum jam to saucepan; stir well.
4. Increase temperature to medium-high and add whiskey to the saucepan; bring to a boil.
5. Serve over bison steaks.

CILANTRO YOGURT SAUCE

Ingredients:

1/2 cup fat-free yogurt, vanilla flavored

1 cup fresh cilantro, chopped

1/8 cup fresh mint leaves

1/2 jalapeño, seeded

1 tablespoon garlic, chopped

1/2 teaspoon cumin

1/2 tablespoon lemon juice

1/4 teaspoon salt

1. In a blender, combine sauce ingredients; puree until smooth.

INDEX